NINH BINH

TRAVEL GUIDE

The Ultimate Pocket Guide to a Thrilling
Vacation, Unveiling Hidden Gems and
Must See Attraction Sites in Ninh Binh,
Vietnam

2023

PATRICIA J PARKS

COPYRIGHT

PATRICIA J. PARKS

TABLE OF CONTENTS

INTRODUCTION

Ninh Binh, a compelling location with a spellbinding fusion of natural beauty, rich history, and cultural heritage, is nestled in the northern region of Vietnam. The mysteries of Ninh Binh, the hidden treasures, and the must-see sites that make this area an exciting holiday destination may all be found with the help of this pocketbook.

Overview of Ninh Binh

Vietnam's Red River Delta contains the province of Ninh Binh. As the "Inland Halong Bay" or the "Halong Bay on Land," it is well-known for its beautiful sceneries made up of imposing limestone karsts, emerald-green rice fields, twisting rivers, and serene countryside. Around 1.5 million people are living in the province, which has a total size of about 1,400 square kilometers.

The area was the capital of Vietnam under the Dinh and early Le dynasties in the 10th and 11th centuries. Ninh Binh has a long and illustrious history. As a consequence, Ninh Binh is rich in history and is home to several old temples, pagodas, and citadels that serve as reminders of its illustrious past.

Why Go to Ninh Binh?

There are many compelling reasons to go to Ninh Binh and discover its marvels. Here are a few examples:

a. ***Natural Beauty:*** Unmatched natural beauty may be found in Ninh Binh's attractive settings. The region provides a tranquil and magical backdrop that will wow you with its towering limestone cliffs, flowing rivers, and green landscape.

b. ***UNESCO World Heritage Sites:*** There are two UNESCO World Heritage Sites in Ninh Binh. Hoa Lu

Ancient Capital, the former capital of Vietnam with historic artifacts and unique architecture, and Trang An Scenic Landscape Complex are two noteworthy karst landscapes with caverns, pagodas, and temples sprinkled among them.

c. ***Adventure & Outdoor Activities:*** Outdoor lovers can find enough to do in Ninh Binh in terms of adventure and outdoor activities. Adventure may be found everywhere, from boat cruises through enigmatic caverns and grottoes to cycling along beautiful paths and trekking in national parks.

d. ***Cultural Immersion:*** Visit historic pagodas, wander through rural communities, and take in lively festivals to fully experience Ninh Binh's rich cultural legacy. Engage with welcoming locals to discover Vietnam as it is.

e. **Delectable Food:** Ninh Binh is well known for its mouthwatering cuisine. Among other delicious foods, indulge in regional specialties like "com chay" (burned rice), "Eel vermicelli soup," and "Mountain snail rice noodle soup."

How to Get to Ninh Binh

There are various ways to get to Ninh Binh, making travel reasonably simple:

a. **By Air:** Noi Bai International Airport in Hanoi, which is around 90 kilometers distant, is the closest significant airport to Ninh Binh. You may go to Ninh Binh from the airport by taxi or private transport, which typically takes two hours.

b. **By Train:** Ho Chi Minh City and Hanoi are both easily accessible from Ninh Binh's railway station, which has its track. Trains are a convenient and lovely method to get to Ninh Binh, enabling you to take in the stunning scenery as you go.

c. **By Bus:** Ninh Binh is accessible by bus from several Vietnamese cities. From Hanoi, there are regular bus services that take between two and three hours to reach the destination, depending on traffic.

d. **By Car:** From Hanoi to Ninh Binh, you may take a cab or rent a car if you prefer the flexibility of a private vehicle. Depending on the amount of traffic, the trip takes around two hours.

Once in Ninh Binh, you may easily see the province's highlights by hiring a local guide, renting a bike or motorcycle, or taking part in pre-planned excursions.

Now that you have a better idea of what Ninh Binh has to offer, it's time to learn more about the top sights, undiscovered treasures, outdoor activities, regional food, shopping alternatives, lodging options, and useful advice that will make your trip to Ninh Binh unique. Join me as we set off on this exciting adventure!

ESSENTIAL TRAVEL INFORMATION

It's crucial to have some key travel information on hand to make the most of your trip to Ninh Binh. The ideal time to travel, visa requirements, currency and money conversion, language and communication, and transit alternatives within Ninh Binh are all topics that are covered in this section.

Ideal Season to Visit Ninh Binh

Although Ninh Binh can be enjoyed all year long, the dry season, which lasts from November to April, is the ideal time to come. The weather is nice throughout this time, with milder temperatures and less rainfall. It is especially advised to go during February and March when the rice fields are in full bloom and provide a breathtaking background for your travels.

It should be noted that Ninh Binh might experience heavy visitor traffic, particularly on weekends and holidays. Consider going on weekdays or during the shoulder seasons between October and May if you want a more tranquil experience.

Visa Requirements

It is crucial to confirm the Vietnam visa requirements before traveling to Ninh Binh. While certain nations are eligible for visas on arrival or waivers, many must get visas in advance. To guarantee a smooth entrance into the nation, it is advised to contact the Vietnamese embassy or consulate in your country or use online visa services.

Obtaining a tourist visa with a longer stay period is advised for those who want to visit many locations in Vietnam. This will allow you plenty of time to visit Vietnam's other amazing locations in addition to Ninh Binh.

Currency & Money Exchange

The Vietnamese Dong (VND) is the country of Vietnam's official currency. Smaller businesses may not take credit cards or foreign currencies, thus it is advised to bring local cash with you for daily costs. In Ninh Binh, ATMs are widely available, making it simple to withdraw money. Larger hotels, eateries, and retail establishments all take major credit cards.

To guarantee fair rates and prevent counterfeit money, it is advised to exchange money at banks or authorized exchange counters. Carrying lesser denomination notes is also a smart idea since some merchants may not have enough change for bigger amounts.

Language & Communication

Vietnamese is the official language of Vietnam. Although English is widely spoken and understood in well-known tourist places, it's helpful to acquire a few fundamental Vietnamese words and phrases to make conversation with locals easier. These words and phrases are helpful:

- **Hello**: Xin chào (sin chow)
- **Thank You**: Cám ơn (kahm uhn)
- **Yes**: Vâng (vung)
- **No**: Không (kohng)
- **Excuse Me**: Xin lỗi (sin loy)
- **I Need Help**: Tôi cần giúp đỡ (toy cahn zyoop duh)

When confronted with language problems, having translation software or a pocket phrasebook might be useful.

Transportation in Ninh Binh

For moving about the province and taking in its attractions, Ninh Binh has a variety of transportation alternatives.

Motorbike or Bicycle Rental: Renting a bike or a motorbike is a common option for tourists in Ninh Binh. You have the flexibility and may go at your speed while exploring. Bicycles are often available for hire at homestays and guesthouses, and you may rent a motorbike from a local store or your lodging provider. If you decide to hire a motorcycle, make sure your driver's license is still in good standing and wear a helmet at all times for safety.

Taxis & Ride-Hailing Apps: Taxis are widely accessible in Ninh Binh, especially in denser populations like Tam Coc and Trang An. Either hail a cab from the street or make arrangements with your hotel for one. In Ninh Binh, popular ride-hailing applications like Grab are also available, offering a practical and dependable form of transportation.

Local Buses: The province of Ninh Binh is connected by a system of local buses. Buses are an inexpensive means of getting between towns and tourist destinations. You may get timetables and directions from the bus terminals or your lodging company.

Private Transfers & Tours: You may choose private shuttles or scheduled excursions if you want a hassle-free experience. Numerous travel companies in Ninh Binh provide day excursions and multi-day packages that include lodging, transportation, and sightseeing tours. You may book private transportation via your hotel or a nearby travel agency.

Since Ninh Binh is a very small province, it is simple to go about by motorcycle, bicycle, or guided excursion since so many sites are nearby. Nevertheless, it's crucial to follow the law, drive carefully, and put your safety first at all times.

You are now ready to plan your trip to Ninh Binh with these vital travel considerations in mind. The next part will take you on a fascinating tour of the province's major attractions, where you'll learn about the delights that this magical place has to offer.

TOP ATTRACTIONS IN NINH BINH

Natural marvels, historical attractions, and cultural icons abound in Ninh Binh. The key attractions that make Ninh Binh a must-visit destination will be covered in this section.

Tam Coc - "Halong Bay on Land"

Tam Coc, often known as "Halong Bay on Land," is one of Ninh Binh's most well-known tourist destinations. This stunning terrain is home to many limestone karsts that majestically rise from the emerald-green Ngo Dong River. A boat cruise that meanders among the karst formations and down the river is the finest way to see Tam Coc. You'll be spellbound by the breathtaking beauty of the surroundings as you cruise across the serene rivers. Tam Coc is especially well-known for its rice fields, which change color depending on the season and provide an entrancing tapestry of colors.

Trang An Scenic Landscape Complex

Trang An Scenic Landscape Complex, another Ninh Binh UNESCO World Heritage Site, is a captivating location that displays the region's natural treasures. This enormous region is made up of limestone karsts, caverns, and verdant valleys that are all linked by a web of rivers and canals.

Join a boat trip that will take you through the captivating Trang An complex, where you can see the magnificent rock formations and pass under low-hanging caverns. Along the route, you'll also pass across historic temples and pagodas tucked away in the lovely surroundings. You may fully enjoy the splendor of Ninh Binh's natural heritage in Trang An, which provides a tranquil and magical experience.

Bai Dinh Pagoda

On the flanks of Dinh Mountain stands the majestic structure known as Bai Dinh Pagoda. This vast Buddhist building not only serves as a spiritual hub but also houses several documents. It is home to the biggest bronze Buddha statue in Southeast Asia, measuring 10 meters in height. With 500 finely carved stone sculptures dotting the complex, Bai Dinh Pagoda also holds the greatest collection of Arhat statues in Vietnam.

Admire the elaborate architecture and serene atmosphere as you explore the majestic temples, pagodas, and pavilions that make up this spectacular complex. Numerous tourists go to the annual Bai Dinh Pagoda Festival, which is celebrated around the Lunar New Year, to take in the lively festivities and customary ceremonies.

Cuc Phuong National Park

A trip to Cuc Phuong National Park is essential for nature lovers. Cuc Phuong, Vietnam's first national park, is a biodiversity hotspot because it is home to a wide variety of plants and animals.

Explore the beautiful woods of the park, hike along its well-indicated paths, and see unusual creatures including langurs, gibbons, and a variety of bird species. In addition, the park is renowned for its venerable trees, some of which are said to be more than a thousand years old.

The park's Endangered Primate Rescue Center is devoted to the preservation and recovery of primates and provides visitors with the opportunity to see and learn about these amazing animals up close. For those who like the outdoors, Cuc Phuong National Park provides a tranquil haven where they may commune with Ninh Binh's abundant natural beauty.

Hoa Lu Ancient Capital

Explore the historic ruins of Hoa Lu, the former capital of Vietnam, and go back in time. In the 10th and 11th centuries, this UNESCO World Heritage Site functioned as the nation's governmental and cultural hub. Although the ancient buildings are no longer standing, the temples and citadels that are still standing provide a look into the region's rich past.

The primary attractions of Hoa Lu are the Dinh and Le temples, which are devoted to the Dinh and Le dynasties that once controlled Vietnam. The complex's exquisite carvings, stone sculptures, and lavishly adorned temples all showcase the period's architectural design as you explore it. For history fans and culture lovers, Hoa Lu is a fascinating visit because of its tranquil settings and historical relevance.

Van Long Nature Reserve

A tranquil haven from busy daily life, Van Long Nature Reserve is a beautiful wetland region. This serene setting is known as the "Bay Without Waves," and it has a sizable body of calm water that is encircled by limestone mountains and lush flora.

Embrace the unspoiled beauty of the region by taking a boat cruise around the reserve. You'll get the opportunity to see a variety of bird species as you soar along the lake, including the endangered Delacour's langur, which is native to the area. The Van Long Nature Reserve is a retreat for individuals seeking peace and solitude as well as a utopia for those who enjoy the outdoors.

Phat Diem Cathedral

The Phat Diem Cathedral is a one-of-a-kind construction that combines European and Vietnamese design elements. The cathedral, which is situated in the Kim Son District, is notable for its elaborate architecture and magnificence. Aside from the main church, the complex also includes bell towers, chapels, and stone sculptures.

The cathedral's interior is filled with exquisite woodwork and ornate paintings, which contribute to the tranquil and uplifting ambiance. The cathedral is a cultural icon that exhibits the harmonious synthesis of Eastern and Western architectural elements in addition to being a place of prayer.

Bich Dong Pagoda

A hidden treasure in Ninh Binh, Bich Dong Pagoda is tucked away in a verdant setting. The pagoda, which has three floors and is carved into the side of a mountain, provides breathtaking views of the surrounding area.

There are many stone stairs to climb, as well as gorgeous gardens and old trees, on the way to the pagoda. You'll be rewarded for climbing with breathtaking views and a tranquil atmosphere. Each of the three temples in the pagoda complex is embellished with elaborate carvings and vibrant decorations. A quiet haven of peace and spiritual contemplation, Bich Dong Pagoda offers a calm retreat from the outer world.

Thung Nham Bird Garden

Visits to Thung Nham Bird Garden are a must for wildlife enthusiasts and avian aficionados. This ecological location, which is located in Ninh Hai Commune, is home to a wide variety of bird species. Take a boat trip through the bird garden to see groups of birds nesting in the lush foliage and flying over the calm waters. Numerous bird species, such as herons, egrets, storks, and kingfishers, will be seen.

The intriguing caverns of Thung Nham Bird Garden, such as But Cave and Vai Gioi Cave, are famous for their magnificent stalactites and stalagmites. At Thung Nham Bird Garden, take in the splendor of nature and consider how delicately ecosystems are balanced.

Kenh Ga Floating Village

The Kenh Ga Floating Village, which is situated on the banks of the Hoang Long River, provides a fascinating look into the way of life in the neighborhood. This charming community, which includes homes, businesses, and even a floating church, is constructed on rafts and boats.

Explore the community on a boat trip to see how the people, who live off of fishing and aquaculture, go about their everyday lives. You will be surrounded by magnificent limestone karsts and rich vegetation as you go along the streams. A real and immersive experience is provided by the peace and simplicity of Kenh Ga Floating Village, which offers a fascinating contrast to the hectic city life.

The natural splendor, extensive history, and rich cultural legacy of Ninh Binh are all on display at these top tourist destinations. Ninh Binh provides a tapestry of experiences that will leave you in amazement, from the stunning scenery of Tam Coc and Trang An to the historic temples of Bai Dinh and Hoa Lu. Discover the beauties of nature, unearth historical mysteries, and enjoy the colorful culture of this captivating location.

HIDDEN GEMS IN NINH BINH

Although Ninh Binh is well known for its well-liked attractions, the province also has a wealth of undiscovered treasures that are just waiting to be found. This section will focus on a few of these less well-known but no less alluring locations that provide a distinctive and off-the-beaten-path experience.

Hang Mua Peak

Visit Hang Mua Peak for amazing 360-degree views of Ninh Binh's gorgeous sceneries. This hidden treasure, which can be found in Khe Dau Ha Village, provides a difficult yet rewarding hike. Reach the top by climbing the 500 stone stairs, where you'll be rewarded with stunning views of Tam Coc's limestone karsts, flowing rivers, and lush green fields. Particularly at dawn or dusk, the panoramic view from the summit is simply stunning.

A building in the form of a dragon is another element of Hang Mua Peak that gives the location a mysterious air. Take your time to enjoy the natural tranquility and beauty that make Ninh Binh's Hang Mua Peak a must-see hidden treasure.

Thien Ha Cave

Explore the magical realm of Thien Ha Cave, an undiscovered treasure situated in Son Ha Commune. By using a boat to go down the cave's subterranean river, you may have a unique and immersive experience.

You'll be amazed by the magnificent stalactites and stalagmites that decorate the cave's interior as you float through the pristine water. The cave is renowned for its stunning "fairy well," a natural skylight that casts a mellow glow across the cavern. You will embark on a remarkable discovery of

Ninh Binh's undiscovered riches throughout your trek into Thien Ha Cave, which is an ethereal experience.

Van Long Wetland Nature Reserve

Van Long Wetland Nature Reserve is a peaceful haven where you may escape the masses. This undiscovered treasure is a tranquil retreat that provides a pleasant and genuine experience, yet is often ignored by visitors. Take a small rowboat out on the quiet sea, where you'll be surrounded by soaring limestone karsts and luscious vegetation.

Van Long is recognized for having a diverse range of wildlife, including the uncommon and endangered Delacour's langur. As you float through this gorgeous marsh, keep a lookout for animal sightings. Van Long Wetland Environment Reserve is a hidden treasure that environment lovers and bird enthusiasts should not miss because of its tranquility and unspoiled beauty.

Hoa Lu Tam Coc Biking Trail

The Hoa Lu Tam Coc Biking Trail provides a unique approach to discovering the breathtaking scenery of Ninh Binh for those looking for an energetic experience. Take a picturesque ride through villages, rice fields, and the countryside by renting a bicycle.

You can take your time admiring Ninh Binh's splendor as the walk leads you through lovely settings. You'll travel through little towns along the road where you may see how the hospitable locals go about their everyday lives. You may immerse yourself in the local culture and take in the serene beauty of the countryside on the Hoa Lu Tam Coc Biking Trail.

Am Tien Cave

The mysterious Am Tien Cave is hidden among Ninh Binh's limestone highlands. This undiscovered treasure is renowned for its serene environment and ethereal beauty. You'll need to travel through a dense forest to get to the cave, which will make the trip more adventurous. Beautiful stalactite formations will meet you as you approach the cave and sparkle in the dim light. The cave also has a natural pond that is surrounded by lush flora and a peaceful atmosphere. In the center of Ninh Binh's natural treasures, Am Tien Cave is a secret haven that provides a tranquil escape and a chance for reflection.

Thung Nang - Sunshine Valley

A hidden jewel that exemplifies the serene allure of Ninh Binh's countryside is Thung Nang, also known as Sunshine Valley. This less popular option to Tam Coc and Trang An provides a more tranquil and personal experience.

Take a boat journey down the narrow rivers that are bordered by lush rice fields and limestone karsts. Thung Nang radiates serenity, enabling you to lose yourself in the grandeur of nature and take in its soothing noises. Thung Nang is a hidden gem that offers a break from the busy tourist areas because of its unspoiled surroundings and tranquil environment.

Thung Nham Eco-Tourism Complex

A hidden haven, Thung Nham Eco-Tourism Complex provides a perfect fusion of natural beauties and cultural treasures. This complex has a beautiful bird garden, caverns, and several limestone mountains. Take a boat trip across the serene rivers to see the karst formations in the area's stunning natural splendor.

Take a tour of the caverns, including the alluring But Cave, which is decorated with stalactites and stalagmites. A lively bird garden where you can see several bird species in their natural environment is also located at Thung Nham. The Thung Nham Eco-Tourism Complex is a well-kept secret that provides a unique and enthralling experience thanks to the mix of nature, caverns, and wildlife.

But Cave (Dong But)

But Cave often referred to as Dong But, is a well-kept secret situated in the Ninh Binh foothills. This fascinating cave is known for its stunning stalactite formations and distinctive rock formations that resemble different animals and items. Explore the complex network of chambers in the cave and take in the natural marvels that have been carved out over millions of years.

The cave's entrance is embellished with a lovely stone arch, which adds to its allure. You will be mesmerized by the fantastical beauty and the minute nuances that nature has crafted as you explore But Cave more. But for those prepared to walk off the usual route, the Cave is a hidden treasure that provides an unforgettable experience.

The opportunity to explore the province's lesser-known treasures is provided by these undiscovered jewels in Ninh Binh. The panoramic vistas of Hang Mua Peak and the ethereal grandeur of Am Tien Cave are just two examples of the hidden gems that each provide a unique and alluring experience. As you learn more about Ninh Binh's undiscovered beauties, embrace the thrill of adventure and exploration.

OUTDOOR ACTIVITIES IN NINH BINH

Outdoor lovers will love Ninh Binh's natural beauty and variety of scenery. Ninh Binh provides a broad variety of outdoor activities that appeal to varied interests and degrees of daring, from boat cruises along meandering rivers to intense rock climbing expeditions. This section will look at some of the exhilarating activities that let you take in Ninh Binh's gorgeous surroundings.

Cruises & Boat Tours

One of the most well-liked activities in Ninh Binh is taking a boat trip or cruise to see the gorgeous rivers and limestone karsts of the region. The two primary locations for boat cruises are Tam Coc and Trang An. Embark on a leisurely voyage along meandering rivers while being surrounded by high cliffs and rich vegetation by boarding a traditional

35

sampan or rowboat. The boatmen, who are often locals, expertly handle the streams as they take you to secret caverns and grottoes along the way.

You will be enthralled by the grand majesty of the landscapes that appear before you as you glide across the calm seas. The natural beauties of Ninh Binh may be completely appreciated via boat cruises, which provide a distinctive viewpoint.

Biking & Cycling

Cycling and biking are excellent ways to discover Ninh Binh's picturesque countryside at your own pace. Set out on a two-wheeled adventure by renting a bicycle from one of the neighborhood stores or your lodging. The Hoa Lu Tam Coc Biking Trail is a well-liked route that passes through verdant rice fields, small towns, and picturesque settings.

As you pedal along the peaceful roads, taking in the beauty of the countryside, feel the soft breeze on your face. You may also go farther afield and explore the neighboring regions, finding undiscovered attractions and getting to know the warm-hearted inhabitants along the way. In Ninh Binh, motorcycling and cycling provide a feeling of independence and a deeper connection to the environment.

Hiking & Trekking

The varied terrain and breathtaking scenery of Ninh Binh provide good chances for hikers and trekkers. A variety of routes in Cuc Phuong National Park lead to stunning overlooks while winding through lush woods and past old trees, making it a favorite location for nature enthusiasts.

You'll get the opportunity to see unusual creatures, such as langurs and numerous bird species, while you stroll around the park. Another trekking option is the

500-step climb to the summit of Hang Mua Peak, where you may take in the expansive views of the surrounding karst formations and rice fields. You'll be rewarded with breathtaking views at every turn, making the effort worthwhile. Get your hiking boots on and get ready to go around Ninh Binh's natural treasures.

Bird Watching

Due to its vast biodiversity and quantity of avian species, Ninh Binh is a haven for bird watchers. The Thung Nham Bird Garden and the Van Long Wetland Nature Reserve are excellent places to see birds.

Armed with a pair of binoculars and a sharp eye, go out on your own or sign up for a guided tour. You'll get the chance to see a variety of bird species as you explore the marshes and canals, including herons, egrets, kingfishers, and even the endangered Delacour's langur. Ninh Binh is a paradise for birds because of its tranquil settings and natural ecosystems, offering nature lovers an outstanding bird-watching experience.

Rock Climbing

The limestone cliffs of Ninh Binh provide a unique chance for rock climbers. Because of their magnificent karst structures, climbers love the Tam Coc and Trang An regions. For both novice and expert climbers, the cliffs provide a range of difficulties and routes.

Ninh Binh's rock climbing locations provide a thrilling experience and an opportunity to test your abilities against the vertical walls, whether you're an experienced climber or a novice to the sport. Engage with local climbing guides and outfitters to ensure a wonderful climbing expedition in the middle of Ninh Binh's natural marvels. They can provide equipment and instruction.

Kayaking & Canoeing

Kayaking and canoeing are fantastic choices for anyone looking for a more active water experience in Ninh Binh. Ninh Binh's tranquil canals and meandering rivers provide the ideal backdrop for canoeing amid stunning scenery. Join a guided kayaking trip for a more immersive experience, or rent a kayak or canoe and go out on your own to explore the Tam Coc or Trang An region.

You can explore unexplored caverns, see how local fishermen live their lives, and be in awe of the limestone karsts that rise from the water's edge as you paddle along the lake. Ninh Binh's kayaking and canoeing provide a unique viewpoint and an engaging method to take in the region's natural splendor.

Ninh Binh has enough to offer outdoor lovers of all stripes, whether you want a leisurely boat excursion, an adrenaline-pumping rock climbing activity, or a tranquil bird-watching experience. Take part in the exhilarating outdoor activities Ninh Binh has to offer to immerse yourself in the breathtaking scenery, connect with nature, and make lifelong memories.

LOCAL CUISINE AND DINING

The chance to indulge in the mouth watering native food in Ninh Binh is one of the attractions. The cuisine of Ninh Binh highlights the area's agricultural roots and utilization of seasonal ingredients. The food in Ninh Binh is likely to tempt your taste buds, from traditional specialties to delicious street food. We will look at some of the must-try foods and well-liked restaurants in Ninh Binh in this part.

Traditional Ninh Binh Dishes

Com Chay (Burned Rice): A must-try for foodies is Ninh Binh's distinctive meal, Com Chay. Rice is cooked in this special recipe until the crusty bottom layer appears. A tasty blend of fluffy, soft, and crispy rice is the end product. Com Chay is often served with a variety of sides, including pickled vegetables, grilled pork, fried tofu, and dipping sauces. It's a tasty and filling meal that displays Ninh Binh's creativity in the kitchen.

Eel Vermicelli Soup: With soft eel chunks, vermicelli noodles, and a rich broth prepared from eel bones, Ninh Binh is well-renowned for its eel vermicelli soup, also known as "Mien Luon." Usually, an assortment of spices is used to marinate the eel before it is grilled to perfection. Fresh herbs, bean sprouts, and crispy shallots are then used to garnish the soup, providing still another layer of taste and texture. This meal is popular among both residents and tourists because of the flavorful broth, silky noodles, and meaty eel.

Mountain Snail Rice Noodle Soup: Mountain Snail Rice Noodle Soup, also known as "Bun Oc" locally, is another delicacy of Ninh Binh and consists of rice noodles served in a savory broth with soft mountain snails, herbs, and vegetables. To assure their softness and flavor, the snails are carefully chosen and processed. Lemongrass, ginger, and chile are often included in the broth's preparation because they give it a unique taste and scent. A fascinating dining experience, Bun Oc highlights the distinctive tastes of Ninh Binh.

Goat Meat Dishes: Goat meat dishes, a specialty of the area, are well-known in Ninh Binh. Goat meat is tasty and soft, and it may be grilled, stir-fried, or braised in a variety of ways. The "Thit De Nuong," or grilled goat meat, is marinated in a blend of herbs and spices before being cooked over an open flame, producing flavorful and juicy flesh. "De Nau Ruou," a slow-cooked stew with flavorful herbs and spices and soft bits of goat flesh, is another traditional recipe using goat meat. Dishes made with goat meat give a distinctive and mouthwatering flavor to Ninh Binh's culinary history.

Popular Restaurants and Food Stalls

Chookie's: Ninh Binh's Chookie's is a well-regarded eatery with a stellar reputation for its delectable Vietnamese food and friendly service. Local favorites including Com Chay, Eel Vermicelli Soup, and Mountain Snail Rice Noodle Soup are among the traditional meals on the menu. Chookie's takes pleasure in utilizing local, fresh ingredients to make meals that are savory and genuine. Both residents and visitors like it because of the welcoming setting and helpful personnel.

Hoa Lu Restaurant: In Ninh Binh, there is a reputable restaurant called Hoa Lu Restaurant that serves a variety of Vietnamese cuisine. The eatery is renowned for its broad menu, which includes both traditional foods from the area and well-known Vietnamese dishes. Diners may enjoy meals like Fish Cooked in Clay Pot, Stir-fried Morning Glory, and Grilled Goat Meat. The restaurant is a terrific spot to spend a pleasant lunch because of its roomy, cozy atmosphere and excellent service.

Street Food Stalls: Ninh Binh is renowned for having a thriving street food culture. You may discover a ton of food booths and merchants selling a wide range of delectable foods all across the province. You may try delectable street cuisines like Banh Xeo (Vietnamese crepes), Banh Mi (Vietnamese baguette sandwiches), and Che (Vietnamese sweet desserts) on the streets of Ninh Binh City or in the busy Tam Coc neighborhood.

You will enjoy the tastes of Ninh Binh while immersing yourself in the local culture at these street food stands, which provide a distinctive and genuine gastronomic experience.

SHOPPING IN NINH BINH

More than merely beautiful scenery and cultural attractions, Ninh Binh is a shopper's paradise. Ninh Binh offers a unique shopping experience that enables tourists to appreciate the local culture and bring home significant gifts thanks to its thriving local markets and rich legacy of handicrafts. This section will focus on Ninh Binh's retail environment, emphasizing the vibrant neighborhood markets and the wonderful trinkets and crafts that showcase the region's cultural legacy.

Regional Markets

Discovering the variety of goods available at Ninh Binh's markets is an engaging opportunity to interact with the locals, learn about their way of life, and connect with the community. Two notable marketplaces that provide a genuine shopping experience are listed below:

Ninh Binh Market: Ninh Binh Market, which is located in the center of Ninh Binh City, is a busy place where residents and tourists come together to purchase and sell a variety of things. The market has a lively environment because of its brilliant combination of colors, noises, and fragrances. You may discover a huge selection of goods here, such as fresh fruits, vegetables, meats, seafood, spices, and home items. The Ninh Binh Market is a great spot to get a taste of the local cuisine, see city life, and get immersed in the culture of the area. Don't pass up the chance to sample the traditional snacks and street cuisine that local sellers are selling.

Tam Coc Market: Tam Coc Market is a modest yet bustling market that highlights the allure of country life and is located in the picturesque Tam Coc region. The market mainly serves the neighborhood, but it also draws visitors searching for trinkets and regional goods. Fresh vegetables, food, clothing, and handcrafted handicrafts are among the products sold in Tam Coc Market. It is especially well-known for its traditional bamboo crafts, lacquerware, and embroidered goods. You may converse with welcoming sellers, see their workmanship, and learn about regional customs as you wander around the market.

Souvenirs & Handicrafts

The rich cultural legacy of Ninh Binh is strongly ingrained in the province's famed traditional handicrafts. Ninh Binh provides a broad variety of distinctive and significant gifts, including delicate needlework, superb lacquerware, and bamboo crafts. The following are some classic crafts to keep an eye out for:

Embroidery: A historical craft with a specific position in Ninh Binh's cultural heritage is embroidery. Silk threads are used by expert craftspeople to painstakingly sew beautiful designs and motifs onto a variety of materials, including tablecloths, wall hangings, garments, and accessories.

Ninh Binh needlework is renowned for its vivid colors and intricate patterns, which often include motifs from local mythology and environment. Each needlework item is a labor of love and a representation of the skill that has been handed down through the generations. You may support regional craftsmen and carry a piece of Ninh Binh's creative legacy home by buying embroidered goods as souvenirs.

Lacquerware: Another ancient art that is thriving in Ninh Binh is lacquerware. Using many coats of lacquer, the artists cover wooden bowls, trays, vases, and ornamental items. Beautiful and long-lasting works of art are created by delicately hand-painting intricate patterns and motifs onto the lacquer surface. Lacquerware-making calls for perseverance, expertise, and a thorough knowledge of the materials. Each item is distinctive and displays the inventiveness and meticulousness of the regional craftspeople. In addition to adding a sense of refinement to your house, purchasing lacquerware as gifts helps to preserve this age-old technique.

Bamboo Products: Because of its adaptability and sustainability, bamboo flourishes in Ninh Binh's natural setting. Bamboo is used by local artists to make a variety of handicrafts, such as baskets, hats, fans, kitchenware, and ornamental objects. Bamboo items showcase the eco-friendly procedures used in the region and the creativity of the artisans.

Each product incorporates elaborate patterns and useful elements while showcasing the strength and beauty of bamboo in its natural state. You may help preserve this environmentally beneficial industry and support local craftspeople by buying bamboo souvenirs.

Make sure to stop by the neighborhood markets while touring Ninh Binh's retail scene so you can take in the lively ambiance and speak with the welcoming merchants. Look for distinctive gifts that showcase the creative legacy of the region, such as embroidered goods, lacquerware, and bamboo crafts. Each purchase helps the neighborhood craftspeople who have devoted their lives to maintaining these traditional crafts while also bringing a piece of Ninh Binh home with you.

ACCOMMODATION OPTIONS

Numerous lodging choices are available in Ninh Binh to accommodate a variety of tastes and price ranges. Whether you're searching for opulent resorts, cozy motels, or memorable homestays, many options might meet your requirements. We shall examine two prominent forms of lodging in Ninh Binh in this section: hotels and resorts and guesthouses and homestays.

Resorts and Hotels

There are several hotels and resorts in Ninh Binh that provide cozy lodgings and contemporary conveniences. Listed below are a few factors that make hotels and resorts popular with tourists:

Range of Options: A variety of hotels and resorts are available in Ninh Binh to suit various needs and interests. Every kind of tourist may find accommodations, from opulent resorts tucked away in stunning scenery to affordable lodging options in prime areas. There are many alternatives available, whether you're looking for a peaceful vacation or a base for visiting the province's attractions.

Modern Amenities: To provide a pleasant stay, hotels and resorts in Ninh Binh are furnished with contemporary conveniences. There are often amenities like swimming pools, spas, workout facilities, and on-site dining options. After a day of touring, you may unwind and revitalize in the pool, indulge yourself in a spa treatment, or enjoy delectable regional and international cuisines without leaving the property.

Scenic Locations: The gorgeous natural scenery of Ninh Binh province is where you'll find a lot of the area's hotels and resorts. Picture waking up to stunning vistas of limestone karsts, verdant farms, or serene rivers. Your visit to Ninh Binh will be even more unforgettable thanks to these beautiful spots, which provide a peaceful atmosphere and a chance to commune with nature.

Professional Service: Ninh Binh's hotels and resorts take pleasure in their commitment to providing its visitors with prompt, courteous service. The competent personnel can suggest local sights, restaurants, and transportation since they are familiar with the region. The team is committed to making your stay comfortable and pleasant, whether you require help planning trips or have particular demands.

Guesthouses & Homestays

Consider staying at guesthouses or homestays for a more authentic experience and an opportunity to engage with the local culture. Guesthouses and homestays are popular lodging choices in Ninh Binh for the following explanations:

Authentic   Cultural   Experience:
Guesthouses and homestays provide a genuine and personal experience that let you fully immerse yourself in the community. You'll have the chance to speak with welcoming hosts, discover more about their way of life, and develop an understanding of regional traditions and customs. It's an opportunity to meet interesting people and enjoy the warm hospitality of the locals.

Cosy and Welcoming Atmosphere: In a more personal environment, guesthouses and homestays often provide pleasant and comfortable lodging. The decor of the rooms often has a personal touch, expressing the host's sense of style. You will feel at home and like a member of the family thanks to the warm and welcoming ambiance.

Authentic Home-Cooked Meals: The chance to have real home-cooked meals is one of the benefits of staying in guesthouses and homestays. The hosts often cook meals utilizing items from their community and tried-and-true recipes. It's an opportunity to sample local food from Ninh Binh and revel in its delectable treats.

Local Knowledge & Recommendations: You may benefit from the hosts' local expertise when you stay in guesthouses and homestays. They may provide insightful information on the top tourist destinations, undiscovered jewels, and off-the-beaten-path activities. You may learn about Ninh Binh from a local's viewpoint and find lesser-known gems by following their suggestions.

Ninh Binh provides a range of lodging alternatives to enrich your stay, whether you prefer the ease and comfort of hotels and resorts or the genuine cultural experience of guesthouses and homestays. A guesthouse or homestay offers an immersive cultural experience, a comfortable setting, and genuine cuisine; a hotel or resort offers contemporary facilities, beautiful settings, and attentive service. Whatever route you choose, Ninh Binh's captivating province is certain to provide somewhere for you to unwind, revive, and create priceless memories.

DAY TRIPS FROM NINH BINH

While Ninh Binh itself has a ton of attractions and things to do, the area around it is also home to many places that are great for day excursions. These day tours provide you the chance to see the many natural settings, historic locations, and cultural gems outside of Ninh Binh. We'll showcase a few of the most well-liked day trip locations that are accessible from Ninh Binh in this section.

Hanoi

The capital of Vietnam, Hanoi, is an excellent day trip location and is situated around 90 kilometers north of Ninh Binh. Hanoi is a thriving metropolis where old-world elegance and contemporary convenience coexist. Discover the Old Quarter's quaint streets and vibrant marketplaces, go to Hoan Kiem Lake and Ngoc Son Temple, and get to know the city's fascinating past and vibrant present. Don't pass up the opportunity to sample the famed street cuisine of Hanoi, which is recognized for its distinctive tastes.

Ha Long Bay

If you get the chance, you should visit Ha Long Bay, which is a natural marvel and a UNESCO World Heritage Site. Ha Long Bay, which is around 150 kilometers east of Ninh Binh, is renowned for its stunning beauty, including green seas and towering limestone islets. Cruise the bay, take in the breathtaking karst landforms, and discover obscure caverns and grottoes. It's a surreal experience that will make you marvel at the beauty of nature.

Perfume Pagoda (Chua Huong)

The Huong Tich Mountains are home to the Perfume Pagoda, often referred to as Chua Huong, which is a collection of Buddhist temples and shrines. The Perfume Pagoda, which is about 70 kilometers southwest of Ninh Binh, is a well-known pilgrimage destination and a location of immense spiritual value. You must first take a picturesque boat trip down the Yen Stream to get to the pagoda, and then climb up to the main complex. Along with being an opportunity to experience religion, the trek offers a chance to fully appreciate the region's breathtaking scenery.

Phat Diem Stone Cathedral

The stunning architectural marvel known as Phat Diem Stone Cathedral is located around 30 kilometers southwest of Ninh Binh. The cathedral was constructed in the late 19th century and combines pagoda and church components with Vietnamese and European architectural styles. There is a major cathedral, a bell tower, several chapels, and lovely gardens inside the complex. A distinctive cultural and historical experience may be had by seeing Phat Diem Stone Cathedral.

Thung Khe Pass

A visit to Thung Khe Pass is strongly advised for anybody looking for stunning scenery and vistas. Thung Khe Pass, a mountain pass linking Ninh Binh with the province of Hoa Binh, is situated about 90 kilometers northwest of Ninh Binh. The scenic views of mountain ranges, terraced rice fields, and dense woodlands are provided by the meandering route. It's a well-liked location for nature lovers and photographers.

Cuc Phuong National Park

Even while Cuc Phuong National Park is already a well-liked tourist site in Ninh Binh, it also makes for an excellent day trip location for those who love the outdoors. The park, which is the oldest national park in Vietnam and is situated about 45 kilometers west of Ninh Binh, is renowned for its extensive biodiversity. Discover its distinctive flora and animals by hiking its paths, exploring its beautiful woodlands, and going to the Endangered Primate Rescue Center. A wonderful place to get close to nature and fully experience Vietnam's natural splendor is Cuc Phuong National Park.

Tam Dao National Park

Another fantastic destination for a day trip is Tam Dao National Park, which is situated around 140 kilometers northeast of Ninh Binh. The park is well-known for its beautiful scenery, abundant animals, and thick woods. Enjoy the paths for trekking, stop by the Tam Dao Ancient Church, and ascend the mountains for sweeping vistas. Tam Dao National Park provides a welcome respite from the commotion of the city.

Kenh Ga Hot Springs

A day excursion from Ninh Binh to Kenh Ga Hot Springs is the ideal way to unwind and rejuvenate. The hot springs, which are around 25 kilometers northeast of Ninh

Binh City, contain naturally mineral-rich waters that are said to have medicinal benefits. Take a mud bath, relax in the hot springs, and unwind in the serene setting. It's the best method to treat and rejuvenate oneself.

Hoa Luu Ancient Capital of Vietnam

Hoa Lu Ancient Capital is a Ninh Binh site, but it's still important to highlight it as a day trip choice for individuals who wish to learn more about its historical importance. Discover the rich history of the capital throughout the Dinh and Le dynasties by seeing the historic temples. Learn about the myths and lore that have influenced this important historical location.

With this day travel alternative from Ninh Binh, you can have a wide range of experiences, from exploring thriving cities to getting lost in the beauty, culture, and history. These day activities will enhance your Ninh Binh travel experience and leave you with priceless memories of your Vietnam vacation, whether you decide to visit the energetic capital city of Hanoi, set sail on a cruise across Ha Long Bay, or explore the spiritual and natural beauties in the neighborhood.

PRACTICAL TIPS FOR NINH BINH TRAVEL

Being prepared and knowledgeable is essential for a hassle-free and pleasurable vacation to Ninh Binh. This area will provide helpful advice on a variety of travel-related topics, such as safety, packing necessities, cultural etiquette, and handy terminology. These pointers will help you get about the province and make the most of your stay in Ninh Binh.

Safety Tips

Prioritizing your safety and well-being is crucial while visiting Ninh Binh. Observe the following safety advice:

a. ***Stay Hydrated:*** It can be hot and muggy in Ninh Binh, particularly in the summer. It's crucial to keep hydrated during the day by drinking plenty of water. Bring a refillable bottle of water with you and keep it full at all times. Additionally, limit your alcohol intake since it might cause dehydration.

b. ***Follow Safety Guidelines during outdoor activities:*** Follow safety precautions if you want to participate in outdoor activities like riding, hiking, or boating. To protect yourself from the sun and mosquitoes, dress appropriately and use sunscreen and insect repellent. Be careful around water or cliff edges, and stick to the routes and pathways that have been approved. When participating in more distant activities, it's also a good idea to let someone know your intentions and anticipated return time.

c. ***Watch your personal belongings carefully:*** It's crucial to take care of your stuff wherever you go. Especially in busy places or while on public transit, keep a watch on your luggage, wallets, and electronic gadgets. To safeguard your valuables near hand, think about utilizing a money belt or a safe bag. Additionally, it's a good idea to create digital copies of your passport, other forms of identification, and travel insurance in case they are lost or stolen.

Packing Essentials

You may make sure you have everything you need for a relaxing and pleasurable vacation to Ninh Binh by packing sensibly. Here are some things to remember while packing:

a. *Lightweight & Breathable Clothings:* Packing light, breathable clothes made of natural materials like cotton or linen is advised due to Ninh Binh's tropical environment. Choose comfortable, loose-fitting clothing to promote greater ventilation. For sun and rain protection, don't forget to carry a hat, sunglasses, and a lightweight raincoat or umbrella.

b. *Comfortable Footwear*: Pack some comfy shoes since Ninh Binh provides options for outdoor adventure. For activities like hiking, trekking, or exploring caverns, think about packing a durable pair of walking shoes or hiking boots. Bring a pair of flip-flops or sandals for resting by the water or on informal adventures.

c. *Travel Adapter & Power Bank:* In Vietnam, plugs normally have two circular pins and the standard voltage is 220V. Bring a multipurpose travel adapter that can fit several plug types if you want to be sure that you can charge your electrical gadgets. When you're on the road and need to charge your gadgets without access to a power outlet, having a power bank may also be helpful.

d. ***Sunscreen and insect repellent:*** Given the abundance of nature in Ninh Binh, it's crucial to protect oneself from insects and the sun's damaging rays. Bring an effective insect repellent with DEET in your bag to fend off mosquitoes and other biting insects. Even on overcast days, remember to bring sunscreen with a high SPF to shield your skin from the sun's UV rays.

Cultural Etiquette

When visiting Ninh Binh, it is crucial to respect the native way of life. Observe the following cultural etiquette guidelines:

Dress Modestly: Dress modestly while visiting religious or holy locations, particularly, since modesty is valued in Vietnamese culture. Choose apparel with sleeves and knee coverage. Respecting regional traditions and customs is shown by dressing conservatively.

Removing Shoes: It's usual to take off your shoes while going inside a person's house, a temple, or a pagoda. Pay heed to warning signs or locals' hints. When in doubt, pay attention to what other people are doing and follow their lead. If you'd rather not go barefoot, don't forget to bring disposable foot coverings or wear socks.

Respectful Behaviour in Religious Sites: Pagodas and temples, as well as other religious buildings, may be found in Ninh Binh. When you go there, be respectful by speaking quietly, abstaining from disruptive conduct, and according to any directions or rules that may be given. If you want to contribute to the site's maintenance, it's also OK to provide a little gift.

Greeting & Interacting With Locals:
The majority of Vietnamese people are kind
and welcoming. A simple grin and nod are
acceptable when meeting natives. Learn a
few simple Vietnamese greetings like "Xin
chào" (Hello) and "Cm n" (Thank you) if you
want to take things a step further. It may
improve your connections with locals and is
often received with warm replies when you
try to converse in their language.

Useful Phrases

Even though English is spoken in certain
tourist locations, being able to communicate
in a few simple Vietnamese words would
tremendously improve your trip to Ninh
Binh. The following are some keywords to
learn:

Greetings & Basic Phrases:

❖ *"Xin chào"* (Hello)
❖ *"Cảm ơn"* (Thank you)
❖ *"Xin lỗi"* (Excuse me/I'm sorry)

- ❖ *"Tôi không hiểu"* (I don't understand)
- ❖ *"Có thể giúp tôi được không?"* (Can you help me?)

Ordering Food:
- ❖ *"Một phần, xin cám ơn"* (One portion, please)
- ❖ *"Cho tôi thêm nước, xin cám ơn"* (Can I have some more water, please?)
- ❖ *"Có món nào ngon nhất?"* (What is the most delicious dish?)
- ❖ *"Tôi ăn chay"* (I am vegetarian)

Asking for Directions:
- ❖ *"Làm ơn chỉ đường tới..."* (Please give me directions to...)
- ❖ *"Bến xe nằm ở đâu?"* (Where is the bus station?)
- ❖ *"Tôi muốn đi đến..."* (I want to go to...)
- ❖ *"Có chỗ nghỉ gần đây không?"* (Is there a nearby accommodation?)

Using and learning these basic words demonstrates respect for the community's way of life and may improve your ability to communicate while visiting Ninh Binh.

You can explore Ninh Binh with ease and have an enjoyable trip if you follow safety precautions, carry just what you need, respect the culture, and learn a few important words. Have fun discovering the natural beauty of the region, getting to know the people, and making memories that will last a lifetime in Ninh Binh.

TOP 10 THINGS TO DO

Travelers seeking adventure and excitement can find plenty of exhilarating activities and attractions in Ninh Binh, a compelling location in Vietnam. Ninh Binh has something for everyone, whether you want to take in the region's rich cultural legacy or explore its stunning scenery. To guarantee an enjoyable and exciting trip, we will highlight the top 10 things to do in Ninh Binh in this area.

1. Take a Boat Tour in Tam Coc

Join a boat journey to Tam Coc, often known as the "Halong Bay on Land," and travel along the Ngo Dong River as you take in the breathtaking karst formations that rise out of the green waters. You pass through three limestone caverns on the boat ride, which is a fascinating and alluring experience. You will be completely engulfed in the grandeur of Ninh Binh's natural surroundings as you float down the canals while being surrounded by high cliffs and green rice farms.

2. Explore Trang An Scenic Landscape Complex

Discover the spectacular limestone mountains, caverns, and rivers of the Trang An Scenic Landscape Complex, a UNESCO World Heritage Site. Get in a rowboat and let the neighborhood rowers guide you through a labyrinth of limestone karsts and caverns. The tranquility of the area and the breathtaking vistas make this an experience that will never be forgotten.

3. Visit Bai Dinh Pagoda

One of the biggest Buddhist pagodas in Vietnam is Bai Dinh Pagoda, a must-see site in Ninh Binh. Investigate the complex, which contains a recently built pagoda as well as an old one. Take in the expansive vistas of the surrounding countryside as you see the complex architectural features and visit the enormous bronze Buddha statue. The tranquil and spiritual ambiance of Bai Dinh Pagoda gives a window into Vietnamese Buddhism.

4. Trek in Cuc Phuong National Park

A trip through Cuc Phuong National Park is an exhilarating experience for nature lovers and those looking for adventure. Discover secret caverns and waterfalls while exploring the varied flora and animals of Vietnam's oldest national park. The park is a haven for nature enthusiasts since it is home to several rare and endangered species. Hike the park's pathways to fully appreciate its beauty and take in the peace of the surrounding landscape.

5. Explore Hoa Lu Ancient Capital

Visit Hoa Lu, the former capital of Vietnam under the Dinh and Le dynasties, and go back in time. Discover the historic structures scattered across the area, such as the Le Dai Hanh and Dinh Tien Hoang temples. Explore the ruins and discover this once-thriving capital's rich history and cultural importance.

6. Experience Van Long Nature Reserve

In the Van Long Nature Reserve, a wetland region renowned for its breathtaking limestone beauty and varied ecology, go on a wildlife adventure. Climb aboard a bamboo sampan and cruise the calm waterways while taking in the many bird species, including the uncommon Delacour's langur. The area also has a wealth of species, making it a sanctuary for photographers and wildlife enthusiasts.

7. Marvel at Phat Diem Cathedral

Visit Phat Diem Cathedral, a masterpiece of Vietnamese and European architecture. This magnificent cathedral has a unique fusion of Gothic components and Vietnamese pagoda-style architecture. Discover the artistically carved wooden pillars, take in the majesty of the main church, and take in the meditative atmosphere of this important holy location.

8. Explore Bich Dong Pagoda

Bich Dong Pagoda is a hidden treasure that provides a serene and scenic getaway since it is tucked away among thick vegetation. To access the pagoda, which has three floors, climb the stone stairs. Each level offers breathtaking views of the surroundings, which include the Ngo Dong River, limestone cliffs, and rice fields. Bich Dong Pagoda is a wonderful location for individuals seeking peace and tranquillity due to its peacefulness and natural beauty.

9. Visit Thung Nham Bird Garden

Thung Nham Bird Garden should not be missed by lovers of nature and birds. Investigate the lovely wetland region to see a variety of bird species in their natural setting. Take a boat trip through the beautiful scenery to see the incredible sight of many birds flying back to their nests at dusk. For those who like the outdoors, Thung Nham Bird Garden provides a serene and uplifting experience.

10. Experience Kenh Ga Floating Village

Experience the distinctive way of life at Kenh Ga Floating Village, where buildings are constructed on rafts and boats. Travel along the Hoang Long River and take in the locals' routine activities like fishing and clam farming. A wonderful and surreal atmosphere is created by the scenic environment of floating homes, limestone cliffs, and rice fields.

Taking part in these exhilarating pursuits and seeing Ninh Binh's finest sights will surely make your trip one to remember. Ninh Binh provides the ideal fusion of scenic beauty, cultural wonder, and adventure, from the enthralling boat cruises in Tam Coc and Trang An to the architectural marvels of Bai Dinh Pagoda and Hoa Lu Ancient Capital. Get ready to be mesmerized by the breathtaking scenery, immersed in the fascinating culture, and make lifelong memories in this magnificent region of Vietnam.

CONCLUSION

With its magnificent scenery, extensive history, and rich cultural legacy, Ninh Binh is a location that genuinely captures the hearts of tourists. Ninh Binh provides a wide variety of activities that suit the interests of any tourist, from the magnificent limestone karsts to the serene rivers and historic temples.

In this travel guide, we've looked into the alluring sights of Ninh Binh, from the well-known boat trips Tam Coc and Trang An to the revered historical landmarks Bai Dinh Pagoda and Hoa Lu Ancient Capital. Additionally, we have made undiscovered attractions like Hang Mua Peak and Thung Nang accessible, presenting chances for special and unforgettable encounters.

Outdoor pursuits including boat trips, cycling, trekking, bird watching, rock climbing, and kayaking have also been covered. These activities let adventurers see Ninh Binh's natural beauty from many angles. Visitors may take part in these activities to fully appreciate the beauty of the region, learn about its varied flora and wildlife, and make lifetime memories.

Ninh Binh has a variety of lodging choices to accommodate different tastes and price ranges. There is an option for every kind of visitor, whether they like to stay in opulent hotels and resorts that provide cutting-edge conveniences and picturesque settings or pick guesthouses and homestays to get a true sense of the local hospitality and culture.

Shopaholics may browse the local markets in Ninh Binh to discover traditional handicrafts including bamboo goods, lacquerware, and needlework. These one-of-a-kind souvenirs not only make beautiful keepsakes but also help to support regional craftsmen and keep traditional crafts alive.

We've included important advice including safety precautions, packing basics, cultural etiquette, and handy language to help you have a smooth and pleasurable vacation. Travelers may explore Ninh Binh with confidence, show respect for the native way of life, and make the most of their visit to this beautiful province by remembering this advice.

In conclusion, Ninh Binh is a place that provides a well-balanced fusion of stunning natural scenery, rich cultural history, and exhilarating adventures. Ninh Binh has much to offer whether you're looking for excitement, peace, or a better grasp of Vietnamese history and culture. Every nook and cranny of Ninh Binh tells a tale and begs for investigation, from the breathtaking scenery of Tam Coc and Trang An to the historic temples and pagodas.

Prepare to be enchanted by the tranquil rivers, captivated by the limestone karsts, and inspired by the rich cultural tapestry that unfolds before your eyes as you go to Ninh Binh. Enjoy the local food, be enthralled by the hidden jewels, and bask in the genuine warmth of the people. The genuinely exciting holiday Ninh Binh offers will leave you with priceless memories and a desire to visit this magnificent location again.

Printed in Great Britain
by Amazon

29116100R00048